HAWKEYE

Daylilies

NORMAN S. TRACK

HAWKEYE
222 Robert Street
Toronto, ON, Canada M5S 2K7

Text and photographs
Copyright © 1997 by HAWKEYE

Canadian Cataloguing in Publication Data
Track, Norman S.
Daylilies

Includes bibliographical references.
ISBN 0-9681703-0-7

1. Daylilies - Pictorial works. 2. Photography,
Artistic. 1. Title.

TR726.D39T72 1997   779' .34   C96-932614-9

Production
Silvio Mattacchione & Co.

Design
Peter A. Graziano Limited

Printed and bound in Canada by
Friesens

All photographs were taken at We're In The Hayfield Now Daylily Gardens, 4704 Pollard Road, Orono, ON, Canada L0B 1M0. All daylilies are tetraploids unless specified in the captions as diploids. Unnamed plants are identified by their daylily (DL) number.

ACKNOWLEDGEMENTS
The author thanks Sandy Cifani, Peter A. Graziano, Donna Krivda, Henry Lorrain, John Lutman, Douglas Lycett, Silvio Mattacchione, Florence Rosberg, Bernie Snitman, Anne Marie Van Nest, Edie Yolles, and Li Zeng.

PERMISSIONS
Wood engravings (p. 9) used with permission from Walter J. Johnson Inc., Norwood, NJ, USA, publishers of the 1974 facsimile edition.

Colour engravings (p. 10) used with permission and from the D.B. Wheldon Library, Special Collections, The University of Western Ontario, London, ON.

Illustration and Chinese text (p. 15) used with permission and from the Cheng Yu-tung East Asian Library, Robarts Library, University of Toronto, Toronto, ON.

... a flower which perisheth at night,

and buddeth at the sunne rising,

... and therefore is called

the Day Lillie, or Lillie for a day.

John Gerard, 1597

Four hundred years ago, John Gerard introduced the name 'Day Lillie' for a plant depicted in his publication *The Herball or Generall Historie of Plants* (facing page). Almost two hundred years later, William Curtis depicted the same two daylily species in coloured engravings in the first two volumes of his *Curtis Botanical Magazine* (following page). Today, Douglas Lycett and Henry Lorrain are breeding daylilies at We're In The Hayfield Now Daylily Gardens. John Gerard would be dumbfounded to see how dramatically the genus has changed.

1 *Lilium non bulbosum.*
The yellow Lillie.

2 *Lilium non bulbosum Phœniceum.*
The Day Lillie.

Publish'd by W Curtis Botanic Garden, Lambeth Marsh.

Publish'd by W. Curtis Botanic Garden, Lambeth Marsh.

Hemerocallis flava (left) and *Hemerocallis fulva.*

I remember clearly that July morning when I first travelled to Orono, Ontario, to photograph daylilies. After a quick walk-about of the extensive Hayfield garden, as we walked back to the farmhouse, Douglas apologized that it was probably going to be a waste of my time. A bad morning. A bad day. After some coffee and breakfast, we set out for another look. "Here, look at the exquisite ruffling on the petals, the distinct water-mark, the lime green throat on this one!" Douglas exclaimed as he examined a new bloom in the first trial bed. It was an incredible flower. I had never seen anything like it before. Each daylily that Douglas or Henry discovered was more remarkable than the previous one.

During the next three hours, I photographed twenty-seven daylilies; we had finished our first day's work. I told Douglas that I hoped that all mornings would be as bad as this one.

By the end of July, I realised how privileged I had been to walk in Douglas and Henry's daylily garden. However, I believe that with privilege comes the responsibility to share the experience with others. Thus, this book celebrates four hundred years of the daylily with a selection of portraits and reflections from Douglas and Henry's magnificent collection of daylilies.

*"*Peeple with large gardens should plant an abundance of daylilies," wrote Chen Hao-Tsu in Flower Mirror (Hua Ching), published in 1688. Traditionally, in China, daylilies were grown for their nutritional and medicinal properties. They were considered a popular cure for melancholy and grief, and it was claimed that if a pregnant woman wore a daylily she would give birth to a son. Written Chinese descriptions of daylilies date from about 3000 BC and the first illustration (facing page) appeared in a Materia Medica (Tu Ching Yen I Pen Tsao) compiled by Kou Tsung-Shih, in AD 1059.*

萱草

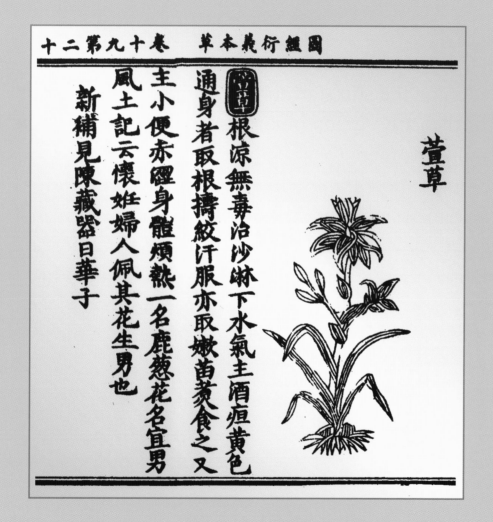

圖經曰

根凉無毒治沙淋下水氣主酒疸黃色

通身者取根擣絞汗服亦取嫩苗煑食之又

主小便赤澁身體煩熱一名鹿蔥花名宜男

風土記云懷姙婦人佩其花生男也

新補見陳藏器日華子

O n a mid-July morning I sat in the hayfield watching the sun start to gently touch the daylilies. For the early-season bloomers today would be 'their day.' I was there to participate in the event and, through photography, extend their grandeur and excitement for an infinite number of days. I walked up and down the rows from one bed to another and realised that in just over a decade this hayfield had been transformed into a daylily paradise.

Hayfield Garden

Daylilies, known scientifically as *Hemerocallis*, made their first appearance in Europe during the 16th century. It is believed that medieval Mongolian settlers planted the yellow *Hemerocallis flava* in Hungary and that the orange *H. fulva* was carried by traders either to Venice or Lisbon. Later in the 16th century, European herbalists - Dodonaeus, Clusius, and Lobelius - described and illustrated both species. They noted that *H. fulva* did not produce seeds. The term 'Day Lillie' first appeared in Gerard's *The Herball or Generall Historie of Plants* (1597). A century later, the pilgrims brought them to America. Settlers carried the sturdier *H. fulva* west

The temple bell stops -
but the sound
keeps coming
out of the flowers.

Basho

with them and it became known as the homestead lily. Daylilies were grown in gardens but with no new introductions they gradually lost their place, in the later 19th century, to the new subtropical bedding plants.

Fortunately, George Yeld, a British schoolmaster with a love for alpine flowers and access to a local nursery, started to hybridise daylilies in 1877. Despite the paucity of breeding material, his original cultivar, "Apricot", received a Certificate of Merit when exhibited in London in June, 1892. Three years later, the 'glorious flower' of the newly acquired *H. aurantiaca* var. *major* set his breeding program off with new

'I have lost my dew-drop', cries the flower to the morning sky that has lost all its stars.

Rabindranath Tagore

vigour. This variety became the parent for many of his best introductions. At this time, independently, Amos Perry, another Englishman, received a collection of *Hemerocallis* from Italy and started breeding. Perry was so meticulous that after seven years of work he introduced only one cultivar. Work over the following four decades produced daylilies with larger, more attractive flowers but were still restricted to shades of orange and yellow.

Broadening the colour spectrum of daylilies was facilitated by the establishment of the Republic of China, in 1911, with their desire for foreign science and technology. Dr. Albert Steward, a Harvard-trained

"Clara Lorrain" is an exhilarating lavender rose 5" flower with a bubbly gold edge on all its segments. A large step forward in gold-edge breeding.

botanist, took up an invitation to teach at Nanjing University in August, 1921. Dr. Steward had agreed to search for new *Hemerocallis* species to assist Dr. Arlow Stout, working at the New York Botanical Garden, in his quest to discover why *H. fulva* was sterile. Three years later, Steward sent three plants of *H. fulva* var. *rosea* to Stout, who established this variety in New York. Subsequently, Stout sent divisions of this variety to Yeld and Perry. Yeld predicted that this beautiful Chinese variety would 'revolutionise the genus.'

Perry, seeing the outstanding results of his initial *rosea* seedlings, realised the validity of Yeld's

Each flower is a soul blossoming out to nature.

Gérard de Nerval

prediction. Besides providing the pink and red colour for daylily breeding, *H. fulva* var. *rosea* also provided the answer to Stout's sterility question. The *rosea* was a diploid, having the normal two sets of chromosomes, while *H. fulva* was a triploid and, therefore, sterile. The new plant material sent by Steward over two decades from China increased significantly the *Hemerocallis* gene pool and allowed Stout to explore other plant characteristics including blooming time, scape height, and number of flowers.

By the 1950's, some daylily breeders felt that the exciting possibilities with diploid plants had been

If a man could pass through Paradise in a dream and have a flower presented to him as a pledge that his soul had really been there, and if he found that flower in his hand when he awoke -
Aye, and what then?

S.T. Coleridge

exhausted and were searching for a 'new rosea' to expand the breeding potential. Several breeders, with a background in tall-bearded irises, cited the example of how average plants were transformed into spectacular plants by doubling the chromosome number. The tall-bearded iris tetraploidy had come, unknowingly, from natural crosses. Tetraploidy can be induced in plants by exposure to colchicine, either by submersion of seeds or treating the mature plants. Orville Fay, an experienced iris breeder, teamed up with Robert Griesbach, whose doctoral dissertation was on *Hemerocallis* seed germination, and together they produced tetraploid daylilies.

The sunlight
on the garden
Hardens and grows
cold,
We cannot cage
the minute
Within its net of gold,
When all is told
We cannot beg
for pardon.

Louis MacNeice

A diploid daylily with a 2.5" melon flower. It has a prominent green heart, a band of chartreuse, and a band of rose. Note the pointed eye patterns and extreme ruffling (DL 104).

They presented their results at the now famous 1961 daylily convention in Chicago. Tetraploids were criticised initially for their coarseness, their lack of finesse, of ruffling, of distinction, and of variety. A small group of breeders saw the enormous potential with tetraploids and started breeding programs. Bill Munson and his mother Ida have been staunch advocates of tetraploids over the last three decades and have made a most significant contribution.

The Munsons did not realise how a gift of some yellow, star-shaped daylilies (an Amos Perry cultivar,

The Infinite has
written its name
on the heavens in
shining stars, and
on the earth in
tender flowers.

Jean Paul Richter

33

A bouquet of pale peach russet flowers with long green throats (DL 124).

Pale amber is a very unusual colour for daylilies. The 5" ruffled flower is equally unusual with its soft green throat and soft rose eye. A fine wire gold edge and delicate diamond dusting are added features (DL 116).

"Queen Mary", 1925), in 1946, was to change
their lives. Bill, still a teenager, planted them along
the driveway of their house in Gainesville, Florida.
The following February they bloomed before the
other perennials and the grand and wonderful yellow
flowers caught young Munson's imagination.
Yearning for more daylilies, he produced his own
plants. The thrill of seeing the first blooms of his own
crosses instilled the desire to breed his own
outstanding daylilies. His collection started with
some of Stout's cultivars. After a period of study, he
started his breeding program by selecting "Show Girl"

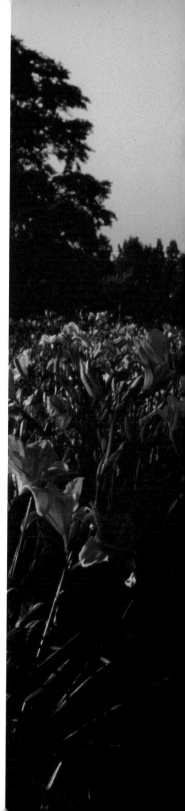

for its clear orchid colour, "Mission Bells" for its excessive bud count, and "Prima Donna" for the broadness of its blooms. After several years, Munson was pleased with the colours of the blooms but purchased some cultivars from New England to bring some hardiness into his developing lines.

Munson, sensing the amazing potential of tetraploidy for daylilies, committed himself to develop such a breeding program. The first year, 5,000 seedlings were treated with colchicine and fewer than 50 plants survived to be planted out. With several years' experience he realised that 90% of the treated seedlings would die and that only 10% of

*Gorgeous flowerets
in the sunlight
shining,
Blossoms flaunting in
the eye of day,
Tremulous leaves,
with soft and
silver lining,
Buds that open only
to decay.*

Henry Wadsworth Longfellow

"Chatelaine Cover Girl" has an unusual 5.5" lavender pink flower with a soft paler watermark and a green throat. The gradations of colour of the stamens and pistil mirror the colours coming out of the heart of the flower. Dots of yellow pollen hover on the stamens and petals. This outstanding daylily was featured on the cover of the Spring 1996 issue of Chatelaine Gardens!

"Glad Gamsby" is an ethereal pale pink peach 5" flower. A lighter edging on the fluted petal segments, a green heart, and a chartreuse throat make it remarkable.

Ye bright
Mosaics! that
with storied
beauty,
The floor
of Nature's
temple
tessellate,
What
numerous
emblems of
instructive
duty
Your forms
create!

Horace Smith

41

the surviving ones would have some degree of tetraploidy. During this time, Quinn Buck, in California,
had succeeded in converting some of Munson's and
other breeders' diploid cultivars into tetraploids.
By serendipity, Buck contacted Munson and offered
him three tetraploids ("SunsetSails"/Munson;
"Sudan"/ Stout; "Big Brassy"/Buck); these plants
formed the foundation of Munson's tetraploid
breeding program.

In 1968, the Munson family moved to
Wimberlyway Gardens with 500 tetraploid seeds
from seven years' work. Seed production skyrocketed
to over 30,000 within four years. After this ten year
investment, Munson very rapidly found major

improvements. Munson's tetraploid daylilies have established standards in form and ruffling in cream to yellow plants, in his purple, lavender and pink lines, and in his introduction of gold-edged flowers.

After three decades of intense work, Munson has written, "the rich colour found in tetraploids; the new patterns and distinctive eyes and edges; the texture; sun resistance; the increased resistance to disease and insects; its added vigour and stamina; all these qualities assure the tetraploid daylily of its rightful place in the world of daylilies."

Douglas Lycett and Henry Lorrain, whose tetraploid and diploid daylilies are featured in this

Day stars!
that ope your
frownless eyes to
twinkle
From rainbow
galaxies of earth's
creation,
And dew-drops
on her lonely altars
sprinkle
As a libation.

Horace Smith

"Louis Lorrain" is a beautiful burgundy 6" flower with a green throat and a unique bluish-grey watermark. A very novel colour combination.

book, are Munson disciples. In 1980, Douglas went with a friend to a nursery to have her select plants for the back garden of his downtown Toronto house. When Eleanor suggested daylilies, Douglas asked, "What is a daylily?" She persuaded him to plant several but none bloomed the first summer. The following summer Douglas ventured out one July morning, saw his first yellow daylily, and fell in love. He knew that he wanted to breed something. He had started with standardbred horses and had considered roses. His experience that July morning made it obvious that it was to be daylilies. To pursue a more pastoral life and the horse breeding, Douglas and

Beauty
in Nature is a quality
which gives
the human senses
a chance
to be skilful.

Bertolt Brecht

A late blooming, very round 5.5"
ruffled, near-white flower - with a
green throat, pale yellow highlights,
soft gold edges, and subtle
diamond dusting. A very special
flower for a very special friend,
"Bernie Bryslan".

Next Spread
"Dark Passage", a very dark
burgundy purple ruffled flower,
appears to be black in the shade.
Notice the ripe pollen on the petals
which have a slight silver edge. The
green on the stamens makes them
look suspended above the green
throat. Amazing branching and
bud count. Very thrilling.

"Absolutely Fabulous" is an
exciting, very ruffled, consistent
double 3" flower. This diploid
daylily displays delicate creamy
peach flowers blessed with vibrant
wine burgundy eyes and edging
on some of the segments.

Henry moved, during 1984, to a five hectare farm
90 km east of Toronto.

Douglas discovered the Gilbert H. Wild & Son
daylily catalogue and started ordering. In 1986,
because of his keen interest and enthusiasm, Shirley
Gene Wild sent him an application for the American
Hemerocallis Society that was to change his life. His
mother's recent death had left him devastated and
directionless. A colour photo of a remarkable dark
lavender tetraploid daylily, a Munson cultivar, looked
back at him from the application's cover.

Douglas realised that it was the best daylily that
he had ever seen. He then knew that this was the
direction to follow. He immediately contacted the

Munsons and went to visit them in Florida. Sensing his sincerity and enthusiasm, Bill Munson gladly became his mentor. Two years later, Henry Lorrain joined Douglas for his annual pilgrimage to the Munsons' Wimberlyway Gardens and returned a daylily convert.

Douglas and Henry had to establish goals for their breeding program. It had to possess sufficient hardiness to survive the Canadian winter; it had to produce flowers exhibiting wide, ruffled petals and sepals, pink and purple colours, and green throats. The first ingredient of a successful, quality breeding program is outstanding breeding stock containing the

Hope smiled when your nativity was cast, Children of Summer!

William Wordsworth

desired traits; they selected and purchased about twenty foundation plants ranging from $50-$300 U.S. per plant. The second ingredient is basic breeding knowledge and experience; the Munsons provided the first, their own crosses the second. The rest would be a matter of time, patience, and luck.

Seeds are harvested from the pods of pollinated plants. The seeds are planted in flats to germinate under lights over the winter. In May, seedlings are lined out and some may bloom the first summer; most bloom after the first winter. After a second winter, surviving plants are scrutinized during the

blooming season and only a small number are picked for the select beds. These selected plants are left for another two years after which they either are ultimately chosen as introductions or dispatched to daylily heaven. Thus, from seedling to introduction is a minimum of 5-6 years. In 1986, 120 seedlings bloomed; in 1996, 10,000 seedlings bloomed. Time, patience and luck!

What started twelve years ago as a hobby in the front-yard garden in Orono has grown to over 10,000 new seedlings yearly and has taken over the hayfield. This book presents an overview of some of the current cultivars of Douglas and Henry's exciting breeding program; some daylilies are already

A lily of a day
Is fairer far in May,
Although it fall and
die that night--
It was the plant and
flower of Light.
In small proportions
we just beauties see;
And in short
measures life may
perfect be.

Ben Jonson

Here come the reds! A gorgeous new daylily - a large, rich dark red ruffled flower (DL 109). Good reds are difficult to breed; thus, this daylily is a major breakthrough.

A miniature rose pink diploid daylily displaying two prominent buds. Note the bubbling, veining, and lighter midribs on the petals (DL 120).

In all things
of Nature
there is
something
of the
marvellous.

Aristotle

63

introduced, and available from them, while others will be coming in the future.

Douglas and Henry's unique contribution to contemporary daylilies speaks dramatically from each photograph and honours the 'Day Lillie' on its four hundredth anniversary.

A brightly coloured, very ruffled, cream flower with a rose eye and some edging on this diploid daylily (DL 127).

This distinguished soft melon pink ruffled flower honours Douglas's mother, "Mary Ethel Lycett", a distinguished public school teacher and principal.

"Pirates Gold Edge" is an outstanding mid-season lavender beacon in the garden. A distinctive 5.5" flower with a green throat. The lighter sepals make it a bi-tone. All the segments are edged in gold. A remarkable parent for pink, purple, and lavender flowers with gold edges.

Next Spread
A large strong amber flower with gold highlights, pink midribs, and prominent ruffling (DL 105).

This enchanting vibrant dark lavender flower has a green heart, a chartreuse throat, and a very large chalky pink watermark which appears on its sepals. The petals and sepals are edged in silver. Dark veining throughout (DL 121).

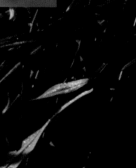

An unusual blending of rose and lavender colours are exhibited in this daylily. The black anthers are an added attraction (DL 111).

The green throat makes this an outstanding daylily. Its 5" ruffled, pink melon flower has a dark eye and a gold edge (DL 117).

Next Spread
A large, heavily ruffled and fluted yellow with pink blush flower. Some ruffling folds back onto the segments. A lovely ribbed and puckered texture (DL 126).

Almost perfect form in this exquisite small pink flower (DL 102). Fine rose veining with tiny ruffles on the petals plus a darker small eye augment the elegance of this diploid daylily.

The most beautiful thing we can experience is the mysterious.

Albert Einstein

Where'er you walk,

cool gales shall fan the glade,

Trees, where you sit, shall crowd

into a shade:

Where'er you tread, the blushing

flow'rs shall rise,

And all things flourish where you

turn your eyes.

Alexander Pope

This distinctive wine purple daylily, "Norman S. Track", will be an important parent for blues. A bluish cast watermark, a chartreuse throat, a green heart, a lavender eye, matching coloured stamens plus veined petals and sepals all contribute to the beauty of this 6" flower.

Next Spread
An exciting rich burgundy flower with wide ruffled petals (DL 128). Very elegant matching stamens and pistil.

Exciting colour contrast and pattern seen in this diploid daylily. Its small cream-peach flower displays a precise plum butterfly eye pattern. The eye is edged and veined in a darker purple (DL 119).

They speak of hope

to the fainting heart,

With a voice of promise

they come and part,

They sleep in dust through

the wintry hours,

They break forth in glory --

bring flowers,

bright flowers!

Felicia Dorothea Hemans

"Yucatan Gold" is an electric gold daylily that has great carrying power in the garden. Its height, extensive branching, and high bud count enhance its garden value.

A very large cream-melon flower (~7") with a puckered texture on its petals and sepals. Its excellent branching and high bud count make this daylily a good garden plant (DL 103).

"Quel Bijou" possesses a distinctive butterfly pattern of lavender etched with plum on its pale yellow petals and sepals. This diploid daylily has 3" flowers and blooms mid-season. What a Gem!

These flowers, which were splendid and sprightly, Waking in the morning's dawn, Will be a pitiful frivolity in the evening, Falling asleep in the night's cold arms.

Pedro Calderón de al Barca

80

Sweet letters of the angel tongue,

I've loved ye long and well,

And never have failed in your

fragrance sweet

To find some secret spell --

A charm that has bound me

with witching power,

For mine is the old belief,

That midst your sweets

and midst your bloom,

There's a soul in every leaf.

Maturin Murray Ballou

"Sans Pareil" is such a beauty! This diploid daylily exhibits cookie-cutter form, round and very ruffled pale cream flowers with pink melon highlights. A beautiful rose-red eye and a green throat enhance its perfect form - truly Without Equal.

A wonderful recurved triangular, full-formed burgundy flower with a green throat. Very elegant matching stamens (DL 122).

The kiss of the sun for pardon,

The song of the birds for mirth;

One is nearer God's Heart

in a garden

Than anywhere else on earth.

Dorothy Frances Gurney

How the universe

is like a bellows!

Empty, yet it gives a supply

that never fails;

The more it is worked,

the more it brings forth.

Lao-tse

*Flowers
worthy of
paradise.*

John Milton

"Endless Glamour" is a pale cream 3.5" flower with a soft pink eye, chartreuse throat and delicate ruffles. This diploid daylily blooms mid-season.

An uncommon colour combination is seen in "Lynne Cooper", a full triangular form of rose red with a sparkling knobby gold edge. A wonderful parent for gold edges.

"Marjorie Mason Hogue" is a tall, late blooming smoky purple beauty with a light purple watermark and a chartreuse throat. Ruffled and fragrant.

"Vera Travis" is a classic flower with wonderful colours. A lovely 5" soft, pale pastel cream-pink flower with a fine wire gold edge and an olive green throat.

Next Spread
The light illuminates the ripe pollen on the anthers of this 2.5" pale melon ruffled diploid daylily (DL 106). The intensity of the dark red eye colour is exceptional. The stamens' filaments exhibit a pronounced colour change.

2 *Lilium non bulbosum Phœnicium.*
The Day Lillie.

'Behold, only for a few days or hours do we bloom',

Exclaimed a lustrous bunch of flowers.

'Yet to be so near to Orcus strikes us not with terror.

At all times we exist and have like thee eternal life.'

Arthur Schopenhauer

Flowers of remarkable size and hue,
Flowers such as Eden never knew.

R.H. Barhan